# Music for the End of Time

Written by *Jen Bryant* • *Illustrated by* Beth Peck

Eerdmans Books for Young Readers

*Grand Rapids, Michigan • Cambridge, U.K.*

In loving memory of my grandparents —
Josephine and Charles
— *J.B.*

For Emma and Anna Rose
— *B.P.*

Text © 2005 Jen Bryant
Illustrations © 2005 Beth Peck
Published in 2005 by Eerdmans Books for Young Readers
An imprint of Wm. B. Eerdmans Publishing Company
255 Jefferson S.E., Grand Rapids, Michigan 49503
P.O. Box 163, Cambridge CB3 9PU U.K.

05  06  07  08  09  10     8  7  6  5  4  3  2  1

Library of Congress Cataloging-in-Publication Data
Bryant, Jennifer.
Music for the end of time / written by Jen Bryant; illustrated by Beth Peck.— 1st ed.
p. cm.
ISBN 0-8028-5229-7 (alk. paper)
1. Messiaen, Olivier, 1908-—Juvenile literature. 2. Composers—France—Biography—Juvenile literature.
3. Messiaen, Olivier, 1908- Quatuor pour la fin du temps—Juvenile literature. I. Peck, Beth. II. Title.
ML3930.M48B79 2005
780'.92—dc22
2004006802

The display type is set in Bergell Plain.
The text type is set in Warnock Pro.
The illustrations were created with charcoal and pastel on paper.
Gayle Brown, Art Director
Matthew Van Zomeren, Graphic Designer

*"In my hour of gloom, when I am suddenly aware of my own futility . . . what is left for me but to seek out the true, lost face of music somewhere off in the forest . . . among the birds."*

— Olivier Messiaen, French composer

The back of the truck was dark and smelled of dirt and sweat. Olivier leaned forward and peered through the slit in the canvas.

Outside, the trees waved their tangled arms in the warm spring breeze. Small birds perched near their nests, calling to their mates. Olivier longed to hear their songs, but the whirring and grinding of the truck's engine drowned out every sound.

They passed through a gate guarded by dogs on leashes and rifle-bearing soldiers.

Olivier clutched his knapsack. Would the soldiers take it away? In the towers, a sign said: Stalag 8A. A cold shiver ran up Olivier's spine . . .

"Raus! Raus! Raus!" German guards hurried
the prisoners off the truck into
the barracks where they gave out uniforms
and mattresses made of straw.

It was dark when the soldiers left. Olivier lay down. A cold draft crept in through the holes in his uniform. His stomach rumbled with hunger. His muscles ached.

Some of the others fell asleep, but Olivier could not shut his eyes. It all seemed like a bad dream . . . He thought about his home in France — his wife, Claire, and his son, Pascal. Would he ever see them again?

"Pssssssst! Hey, you there!" The man in the bunk below tugged on Olivier's sleeve. "What have you got in the knapsack? Some food? Something to eat?"

At the sound of the word "food," those
who were awake crowded around. Olivier
clutched his knapsack. "Come on, then,
show us what you've got."

Slowly, Olivier slid down from the bed.
He untied the leather string and spilled
the contents onto the packed dirt floor.
"Papers! Is that all?" asked the man.
"Yes," replied Olivier. "Just my music, that's all."

"You're a composer?" asked another man.
Olivier nodded. "These are my favorite tunes. I've kept
them with me since the war began. When I read
the notes, I hear music in here," Olivier pointed
to his head. He sighed. "It gives me hope."

The second man nodded. But the first man
pushed the papers roughly away. "Achh!" he said.
"What good is music in a prison camp?"
Scuffling and grumbling, the prisoners
climbed back into their beds.

Olivier gathered the papers carefully.
*That man is right,* he thought. *What good is music in this place?*

All night he lay awake thinking of his home
in Paris. He missed his family, his piano,
his friends, his music students. He missed
the lake and the high peaks behind
his summer house in the Alps. He missed

his backyard where, every morning, the birds
perched in the branches and serenaded him.
He missed music . . . any music. How long
had it been since he had heard even the simplest tune?

Inside, Olivier saw the washrooms and lavatories.
Off to one side, there was a windowless
room no larger than a closet. A single
bulb hung from the ceiling. Olivier squinted.

In the corner sat a small desk with a few
papers scattered across the top.
"It's not large, but it's quiet," said the German.
"As you are a composer, you may come here
for some time each day to work."

Olivier was puzzled. *Why would the Germans
allow me to write music?* he wondered.
The officer's blank look gave him no answer.
"Thank you — Merci!" Olivier managed to say.

Early the next morning, while the others slept,
Olivier strapped the knapsack to his back and slipped
out of the barracks. He walked quickly to the building
and entered the small, dimly lit room.
He sat down at the desk. He stared at the blank
pages. *How should I begin?* he asked himself.

Before the war, the most talented musicians
in Europe had played his tunes. His melodies
filled the grandest cathedrals and the finest
concert halls. But now, everything was different . . .
*Even if I write a beautiful tune, who will
play it? Who will hear it?*

Then, Olivier remembered the nightingale —
how the bird's wild and splendid song
had somehow lifted his spirits.
He picked up a pen and began to write.

The notes spilled quickly onto the page,
then onto the next page and the next.
Olivier lost all track of time.

When, at last, he stepped outside, the sun was already high in the sky. Olivier joined the line of prisoners who waited for their daily meal of soup and bread.

A truck rumbled by and stopped in front of the barracks. "New prisoners," mumbled the man behind him. "Now there will be even less to eat!" But Olivier had barely heard. He was watching two men carrying small black cases leap off the truck. *Musicians!*

That night, Olivier lay awake in his bunk.
His stomach still grumbled and his muscles
still ached, but his head was filled with music.
With his fingers, he tapped out rhythms on his chest.
He had met the two musicians and now he had a plan . . .

For the rest of the summer and into the fall,
Olivier worked hard on his music. Every morning,
he entered the tiny room where he wrote, and wrote,
and wrote. Sometimes, he heard the nightingale
singing from the edge of the woods: *"Eee — oh — lay!"*

In the camp, Olivier met a third musician.
"I'm composing a quartet," he told his three friends
"I will ask the officer if we might be allowed
to play it together."

It was late winter when Olivier finished his tune.
The officer found an old piano with broken keys
and a well-used cello and brought them to the camp.
The four prisoners rehearsed in the washroom.

Then, on January 15, 1941, in the coldest, darkest part of winter, 5,000 prisoners gathered inside Stalag 8A to hear Olivier's tune.
No one talked. No one shuffled their feet or sneezed.

There was absolute silence as the first notes
drifted out from the clarinet and over the crowd.
*"Eee — oh — lay! Eee — oh — lay!"* Like birdsong,
it was wild, beautiful, and full of hope.

# Author's Note

*Music for the End of Time* is based on the true story of French composer Olivier Messiaen (oh-LIV-yay MAYS-yun) who was captured by the Germans during World War II and taken to a prison camp in Gorlitz (now part of Poland). Despite the poor conditions, lack of decent food, warm shelter, or clothing, Messiaen managed to compose his now-famous *Quartet for the End of Time*. With the permission of the camp's young officer, the composer closed himself in a small room in the lavatories and wrote music for a few hours each day. The Germans provided him with a run-down piano and his friend Etienne (ay-tee-YUN) with a used cello. The other two prisoners, Jean (Jawhn), a violinist, and Henri (awn-REE), a clarinetist, brought their instruments with them when they were captured.

On January 15, 1941, more than 5,000 prisoners from all walks of life — plumbers, bankers, doctors, teachers, and farmers — gathered for the debut of Messiaen's work. Soldiers carried the wounded and sick prisoners on stretchers and placed them near the make-shift stage.

The quartet, written in eight parts and lasting nearly a full hour, is based on a passage in the Revelation of St. John where an angel descends and announces: "There will be no more time." Messiaen, a deeply religious man and an avid bird-watcher, frequently incorporated birdcalls in his musical compositions. The opening notes for *Quartet for the End of Time* were, indeed, inspired by a nightingale's song.

Messiaen survived the prison camp. After his release, he returned to the Paris Conservatory where he became one of the most respected and influential composers of the 20th century. When asked about the concert at Stalag 8A, Messiaen recalled: "Never have I been heard with such attention and understanding."